Novels for Students
Volume 9

Staff

Series Editors: Deborah A. Stanley and Ira Mark Milne.

Contributing Editors: Elizabeth Bellalouna, Elizabeth Boden-miller, Sara L. Constantakis, Catherine L. Goldstein, Motoko Fujishiro Huthwaite, Arlene M. Johnson, Angela Y. Jones, Michael L. LaBlanc, Polly Rapp, Erin White.

Research: Victoria B. Cariappa, *Research Team Manager*. Cheryl Warnock, *Research Specialist*. Corrine A. Boland, Tamara Nott, Tracie A. Richardson, *Research Associates*. Timothy Lehnerer, Patricia Love, *Research Assistants*.

Permissions: Maria Franklin, *Permissions Manager*. Margaret A. Chamberlain, Edna Hedblad, *Permissions Specialists*. Erin Bealmear, *Permissions Associate*. Sandra K. Gore, *Permissions Assistant*.

Production: Mary Beth Trimper, *Production Director*. Evi Seoud, *Assistant Production Manager*. Stacy Melson, *Production Assistant*.

Imaging and Multimedia Content Team: Randy Bassett, *Image Database Supervisor*. Robert Duncan, *Imaging Specialist*. Michael Logusz, *Graphic Artist*. Pamela A. Reed, *Imaging Coordinator*. Dean Dauphinais, Robyn V. Young, *Senior Image Editors*. Kelly A. Quin, *Image Editor*.

Product Design Team: Cynthia Baldwin, *Product Design Manager*. Pamela A. E. Galbreath, *Senior Art Director*. Gary Leach, *Graphic Artist*.

Copyright Notice

Since this page cannot legibly accommodate all copyright notices, the acknowledgments constitute an extension of the copyright notice.

While every effort has been made to secure permission to reprint material and to ensure the reliability of the information presented in this publication, Gale Research neither guarantees the accuracy of the data contained herein nor assumes any responsibility for errors, omissions, or discrepancies. Gale accepts no payment for listing; and inclusion in the publication of any organization, agency, institution, publication, service, or individual does not imply endorsement of the editors or publisher. Errors brought to the attention of the publisher and verified to the satisfaction of the publisher will be corrected in future editions.

This publication is a creative work fully protected

by all applicable copyright laws, as well as by misappropriation, trade secret, unfair competition, and other applicable laws. The authors and editors of this work have added value to the underlying factual material herein through one or more of the following: unique and original selection, coordination, expression, arrangement, and classification of the information. All rights to this publication will be vigorously defended.

Copyright © 2000
The Gale Group
27500 Drake Rd.
Farmington Hills, MI 48331-3535

All rights reserved including the right of reproduction in whole or in part in any form.

ISBN 0-7876-3828-5
ISSN 1094-3552

Printed in the United States of America.

10 9 8 7 6 5 4 3 2 1

In the Time of the Butterflies

Julia Alvarez 1994

Introduction

When people think of the Dominican Republic in the twentieth century, two words most often come to mind: Rafael Trujillo. He ruled the island nation from 1930 to 1961. His dictatorship was defined by greed, a rigid control over the Dominican people, and unspeakable brutality. But many would also have people remember another history of the Dominican Republic, a history of brave resistance and immense sacrifice. Two different words come to mind when thinking of this history: Las

Mariposas, or The Butterflies. These were the code names of Minerva, María Teresa, and Patria Mirabal, three sisters who were key members in an underground movement to overthrow Trujillo. On November 25, 1960, the dictator's men ambushed their car and the sisters were beaten to death. Since that time, they have become symbols of courage, dignity, and strength in their country.

In 1994, Julia Alvarez brought the Mirabals' story to an American audience through her novel *In the Time of the Butterflies*. Alvarez's connections to this story run deep, since her own parents were involved in the underground movement and fled to America before being arrested. She does not write a history or a biography, however. She fictionalizes the Mirabal sisters and depicts their lives through the voices she creates for them. She even includes Dedé Mirabal, the only sister to survive, as a voice of the present reflecting on the past. Through her characters, she stresses the need to remember the past, even times of great pain, while also striving for happiness in the present and the future. Perhaps more importantly, she stresses the need to see heroes not as superhuman, but as people who fight their own fears in order to fight injustice.

Author Biography

Alvarez was born in New York City on March 27, 1950, the second of four daughters. Shortly thereafter, the family moved to the Dominican Republic, where her parents were involved in an underground movement to overthrow Dominican dictator Rafael Trujillo. When the movement was discovered, the Alvarez family was forced to flee to escape imprisonment and possible death. They left the Dominican Republic on August 6, 1960, and moved to Queens, New York.

While living in New York, Alvarez had to perfect her English and adjust to life as an immigrant. She was alienated at school and subject to taunting from other students. As a result, she turned to reading for solace. These experiences proved important for her future writing. She writes in "A Brief Account of My Writing Life" for the Appalachian State University Summer Reading Program, "I came into English as a ten-year-old from the Dominican Republic, and I consider this radical uprooting from my culture, my native language, my country, the reason I began writing. 'Language is the only homeland,' Czeslow Milosz once observed, and indeed, English, not the United States, was where I landed and sunk deep roots."

Alvarez began attending a boarding school at age thirteen. By high school, she desired to become a writer. She was encouraged by teachers but not by her family. She explains to Jonathan Bing of *Publishers Weekly* part of her family's reasoning: "I grew up in that generation of women thinking I would keep house. Especially with my Latino background, I wasn't even expected to go to college.... I had never been raised to have a public voice." She pursued her writing interests at Connecticut College, however, where she won two prizes for her poetry in 1968 and 1969. She then attended Middlebury College in Vermont, where she won the Creative Writing Prize and graduated summa cum laude in 1971. She received an M.A. in creative writing from Syracuse University in 1975. While at Syracuse, she won the American Academy of Poetry Prize in 1974.

Between 1975 and 1977, she worked for the Kentucky Arts Commission, conducting poetry workshops throughout the state. In 1978, she worked in a National Endowment for the Arts bilingual program in Delaware and a program for senior citizens in North Carolina. From 1978 to 1988, she taught English and creative writing at a number of institutions. She began teaching at Middlebury College in 1988.

In 1984, she published *Homecoming*, a well-received collection of poetry. Her next major publication, *How the Garcia Girls Lost Their Accents*, appeared in 1991. This highly popular novel details the lives and struggles of four sisters who emigrated from the Dominican Republic to America. In 1994, she published *In the Time of the Butterflies*, which received much critical attention and praise. The following year, she published a second poetry collection entitled *The Other Side: El Otro Lado*. Her novel *!Yo!* appeared in 1997, and a collection of personal essays, *Something to Declare* was published in 1998.

Alvarez married Bill Eichner, an ophthalmologist, in 1989, and she continues to write and teach at Middlebury College.

Plot Summary

Set in the Dominican Republic, *In the Time of the Butterflies* depicts the lives of the Mirabal family between 1938 and 1994. The chapters are narrated by the four Mirabal sisters, Patria, Dedé, Minerva, and María Teresa, or Mate. Alvarez arranges events in roughly chronological order, though she excludes many years from the narrative and gives only brief treatment to the period between 1960 and 1994.

Section I: 1938 to 1946

The novel opens in 1994 with Dedé, the surviving Mirabal sister. She meets with an American woman who has come to interview her about her family. She recalls a time in 1943 when her father, Enrique, was predicting his daughters' futures. He tells Dedé that she will bury them all "in silk and pearls."

The second chapter is narrated by Minerva and depicts events in 1938, 1941, and 1944. Minerva and Patria go to boarding school at Inmaculada Concepción. Minerva befriends a withdrawn girl named Sinita Perozo. Sinita's male family members were murdered for opposing the Dominican dictator, Rafael Trujillo. Minerva is shocked to learn of Trujillo's cruelty, since all Dominican children are taught to revere him. In 1941, the married Trujillo seduces the most beautiful girl in

Minerva's school, Lina Lovatón. After Lina becomes pregnant, Trujillo sends her to live in Miami. In 1944, Minerva, Sinita, and their friends Elsa and Lourdes perform a play for the country's Independence Day celebrations and win the opportunity to perform before Trujillo. During this performance, Sinita points a bow and arrow at Trujillo. Sinita is stopped by Trujillo's son, Ramfis, and Minerva intervenes by having everyone chant "*Viva Trujillo*," or "Long live Trujillo."

The third chapter consists of María Teresa's diary entries between 1945 and 1946. She describes her childhood pleasures, especially clothes. She also talks about Minerva's friendship with Hilda, a revolutionary fighting Trujillo. When Hilda is caught, María Teresa must bury her diary so the police will not find it.

Chapter four is narrated by Patria and begins in 1946. Patria wrestles with the question of whether she should become a nun. Soon, however, she falls in love with Pedrito González, a farmer, and they marry. They have a son and daughter, Nelson and Noris, but their third child is born dead. Grief-stricken, Patria loses her religious faith. She regains her faith, though, when she hears the Virgin Mary speak to her through a church congregation gathered for worship.

Section II: 1948 to 1959

Chapter five opens in 1994 with Dedé telling the interviewer about Virgilio (Lío) Morales. Dedé privately recalls her own romantic interest in Lío when he was a young doctor and revolutionary. The narrative shifts to 1948, when the Mirabals met Lío. Dedé is beginning a romance with her cousin Jaimito, whom she soon marries. Minerva is attracted to Lío's Communist politics, though she never admits it to him. When Lío must flee the country, he asks Dedé to give Minerva a letter asking her to join him in exile. Dedé burns the letter.

Minerva narrates the sixth chapter, which begins in 1949. Three years after graduating Inmaculada, she is bored at home and wants to attend law school. She discovers that her father has four illegitimate daughters and that he has been hiding Lío's letters to her. The family goes to an outdoor party hosted by Trujillo, and Minerva slaps Trujillo when he becomes lewd while they are dancing. It begins to rain, and the Mirabals leave the party, even though it is against the law to do so. Minerva forgets her purse, which contains Lío's letters. Enrique Mirabal is soon arrested. After many weeks, Minerva and her mother secure his release by apologizing to Trujillo personally.

Chapter seven consists of entries from María Teresa's diary between 1953 and 1958. She discusses her father's death in 1953, her romantic dilemmas, Minerva's experiences in law school, and her own experiences at college. Minerva marries Manolo Tavárez, has a daughter, Minou, and earns her law degree, but Trujillo refuses her a license to practice. During the summer, María Teresa stays with Minerva's family. Minerva and Manolo have marital problems until they become involved in an underground movement against Trujillo. They explain the movement to María Teresa and reveal their code names. Minerva is Mariposa, or Butterfly. María Teresa joins them, largely because of her feelings for Leandro Guzmán, or Palomino, a man in the movement. She becomes Mariposa #2. She marries Leandro on February 14, 1958.

Patria narrates chapter eight, which covers 1959. She becomes pregnant and decides to name the child Raúl Ernesto after the Cuban revolutionaries Raúl Castro and Ernesto (Che) Guevara. The movement needs a place to meet, and Patria offers them her farm. Patria goes on a religious retreat. On the fourteenth of June, the retreat is bombed when Trujillo's forces attack rebels hiding in the mountains. Patria watches a boy die. She vows to help in the resistance, and she convinces Pedrito to do the same, though they will lose their farm if they are caught. The resistance names itself the Fourteenth of June Movement.

Section III: 1960

Dedé narrates chapter nine. She tells the interviewer that though she was sympathetic to the movement, she did not get involved in it because Jaimito would not. Dedé recalls that in 1960 she and Jaimito experience serious marital problems, but she stays with him. Minerva, María Teresa, and their husbands are arrested, along with Patria's husband

and son, Nelson. Patria's family loses the farm.

Patria narrates chapter ten, which takes place between January and March, 1960. She lives at her mother's house, which is under constant surveillance. Captain Victor Alicinio Peña, one of Trujillo's top officials, begins to visit the house to keep tabs on the family. Margarita Mirabal, Patria's illegitimate half-sister, also visits with a prison message from María Teresa. Margarita's cousin is a guard in the prison, and the family sends the prisoners items through him. To gain favorable publicity, Trujillo allows Nelson to be released.

Chapter eleven consists of María Teresa's diary entries from March to August, 1960. She is in a cell with Minerva and twenty-two other women, most of whom are non-political criminals. She describes her prison experiences, including the women's routines, means of resistance, and the indignities they suffer. The worst incident María Teresa must endure is being electrically shocked before her husband. Seeing her pain, he agrees to cooperate with Trujillo's men. The Organization of American States sends inspectors to the prison. María Teresa secretly gives one inspector the story of her torture. Soon after, the female political prisoners are released.

Minerva narrates chapter twelve, which occurs between August and November 25, 1960. While under house arrest, she struggles to be her old, courageous self, but finds it hard to do so until faced with adversity. She discovers the hoped-for invasion of the island has been called off and most of the movement disbanded. Later, at a gathering, Trujillo declares that his only two remaining problems are the church and the Mirabal sisters. Manolo and Leandro are transferred to Puerto Plata prison. The sisters must cross isolated mountain roads to get there for visitations. Minerva, María Teresa, Patria, and Rufino de la Cruz travel to the prison on November 25. On the way, they fear an ambush, but they arrive safely. They try calling home before heading back, but the line is busy.

Epilogue

In 1994, Dedé recalls the story of the sisters' and Rufino's deaths. On the road home, they were stopped by soldiers, who beat them to death then pushed them over a cliff in their car. Dedé recalls her slow process of healing and becoming the family spokesperson. She also recalls recently seeing Lío Morales at a reception and discussing the past and the current political situation with him. To Dedé, the Dominican Republic has become "the playground of the Caribbean" rather than its "killing fields." The materialistic young people have forgotten their past. Dedé asks herself, "Was it for this, the sacrifice of the butterflies?"

Characters

American Interviewer

An American woman of Dominican descent, the interviewer comes to speak with Dedé about the family history. She speaks poor Spanish. She strongly resembles Julia Alvarez herself.

Sor Asunción

As the head nun at Inmaculada Concepción, Sor Asunción tends to all of the Mirabal sisters. She prompts Patria to watch for God's call to become a nun.

Don Bernardo

When Chea Mirabal moves to town, Don Bernardo becomes her neighbor. Though his wife, Doña Belén, suffers from senility, he finds time to help the Mirabal family whenever they are in need.

Chea

See Mercedes Reyes de Mirabal

Rufino de la Cruz

Rufino is the Mirabal sisters' favorite

chauffeur, and he is fiercely protective of them. He dies with Patria, Minerva, and María Teresa.

Manuel de Moya

De Moya is Trujillo's Secretary of State, but his actual job is to secure attractive young women for Trujillo. He arranges the meeting between Minerva and Trujillo at the Discovery Day Dance, where she slaps the dictator.

Enriquello

See Manolo Tavárez

Jaime Fernández

Jaimito is the Mirabals' cousin and Dedé's husband. He has little business sense, so he and Dedé suffer through financial hardship. He refuses to allow Dedé to become involved in her sisters' political activities because he fears reprisals. Because of his domineering ways, Dedé almost leaves him in 1960, but they stay married until they divorce in the 1980s. Though blustery, he often proves to have a good heart.

Nelson González

Patria's eldest child, Nelson, enthusiastically joins the underground when he is a young man. He is caught and imprisoned. Trujillo releases him for favorable publicity, and he goes to work for Jaimito on his farm.

Noris González

Noris is Patria's daughter. She goes with her mother to retrieve Nelson from prison.

Pedro González

A gentle, plainspoken farmer, Pedrito is Patria's husband. They meet when she washes his feet during a church ceremony. He loves his family and his land. He risks both, however, when Patria asks him to help in the underground movement. He is imprisoned and loses his farm when caught. After being released, he remarries and regains his land, but he is restless and does not resume farming.

Gringa Dominicana

See American Interviewer

Leandro Guzmán

Leandro, María Teresa's husband, is an engineer and revolutionary, code-named Palomino. He meets María Teresa while delivering guns to Manolo and Minerva's house. He is arrested in 1960. Like the other men, he is tortured. He agrees to help Trujillo's men after watching his wife being tortured by electric shocks. After his wife's death and his release, he follows Manolo for a time, then leaves politics. He becomes a successful builder in the capital, remarries, and has another family.

Hilda

A young revolutionary friend of Minerva's, Hilda must hide at Inmaculada Concepción to escape the police. She is arrested when seen leaving the school.

Jaimito

See Jaime Fernández

El Jefe (The Chief)

See General Rafael Trujillo

Lío

See Virgilio Morales

Lina Lovatón

The most beautiful girl at Inmaculada Concepción, Lina is seduced, impregnated, and then abandoned by Trujillo, whom she loves.

Magdalena

Magdalena befriends and develops a romantic interest in María Teresa while they are in prison together.

Mamá
>*See* Mercedes Reyes de Mirabal

Mariposa (Butterfly) #1
>*See* Minerva Mirabal de Tavárez

Mariposa (Butterfly) #2
>*See* María Teresa Mirabal de Guzmán

Mariposa (Butterfly) #3
>*See* Patria Mercedes Mirabal de González

Mate
>*See* María Teresa Mirabal de Guzmán

Enrique Mirabal

A successful farmer and store owner, Enrique Mirabal is the father of the Mirabal sisters and a man of means who accommodates the Trujillo regime rather than fighting it. Though he loves his children, he is disappointed that he has four daughters and no son. When María Teresa is still a young child, he begins a long-standing affair with another woman and has four daughters with her. He will not allow Minerva to attend law school, and he hides Lío Morales's letters to her. Minerva discovers his secret life, but they reach a truce and she accepts her half-sisters. After Minerva slaps Trujillo at the Discovery Day Dance, Enrique is arrested and kept in jail for weeks. He suffers a heart attack and nearly loses his mind before being released. He dies on December 14, 1953.

Margarita Mirabal

Margarita is the oldest of Enrique Mirabal's illegitimate daughters. She is a pharmacist and arranges for packages to be sent to Minerva and María Teresa in prison.

Dedé Mirabal de Fernández

Dedé is the second-oldest and last surviving Mirabal sister. In her late sixties in 1994, she is a successful life insurance agent. Since her youth, she has been very practical and good with math and business. In 1948, during her courtship with her cousin and eventual husband, Jaimito, she first meets Lío Morales, for whom she holds a secret attraction. She burns Lío's letter to Minerva asking her to go into exile with him. She and Jaimito have three sons, Enrique, Rafael, and David. Because she allows Jaimito to control their business ventures, the family is often in financial trouble. Jaimito forbids her from becoming involved in her sisters' political activities, and she gives in to his wishes because "She had always been the docile middle child, used to following the lead…. Miss Sonrisa, cheerful, compliant. Her life had gotten bound up with a domineering man, and so she shrank from the challenge her sisters were giving her." In 1960, she is unhappy in her marriage and almost leaves Jaimito, but they reconcile, though she still has serious doubts about their union. Once her sisters are arrested, she and Jaimito work hard to care for the family. She is devastated by her sisters' deaths, but she recovers and helps raise her sisters' children. She and Jaimito divorce in the 1980s, and she later survives breast cancer. Since 1960, she has helped keep the memory of her sisters alive.

Media Adaptations

- The rights to a film version of *In the Time of the Butterflies* have been bought by Barnstorm Films and Phoenix Pictures.

Patria Mercedes Mirabal de González

Patria is the oldest and most religious of the Mirabal sisters. Her devotion to her religious pursuits catches the attention of the nuns at Inmaculada Concepción, and Sor Asunción tells Patria to watch for God's call to enter the sisterhood. Instead, Patria finds her call while washing Pedrito González's feet at a religious ceremony. She marries him when she is sixteen, and they quickly have two children, Nelson and Noris. Their third child is stillborn, which devastates them both. The child's death, coupled with her awareness of Trujillo's crimes, even causes Patria to lose her religious faith. She regains this faith, however, when on a pilgrimage. She hears the Virgin Mary speaking not through the Church but through the people themselves. Her religious belief is both transformed and strengthened by this experience.

When Nelson is in his teens, Patria worries about his desire to become involved with his aunts and uncles in the underground movement. Still, she and Pedrito allow the movement to meet on their land, but not in their house. She becomes pregnant again and decides to name the child Raúl Ernesto after the Cuban revolutionaries Raúl Castro and Ernesto (Che) Guevara. Patria becomes more intimately involved with the movement after attending a retreat in the mountains. The retreat is bombed when Trujillo's forces attack underground soldiers hiding in the mountains. Patria watches a teenaged boy be shot to death and feels a sharp kinship with him.

Upon her return home, she convinces Pedrito to hold the movement meetings in their home, which puts their farm at great risk. In 1960, Pedrito and Nelson are arrested and the government confiscates the farm. Patria moves in with her mother. She helps arrange secret contacts with her imprisoned sisters. Her contact is Margarita Mirabal, her illegitimate half-sister, and Patria sees her past rejection of Margarita as shameful. Patria is very adept at convincing Captain Peña to treat the family as well as possible, and she is overjoyed when he helps Nelson secure an early release from prison. Pedrito is not sent to Puerto Plata prison with Manolo and Leandro, but she accompanies her sisters on their final visit there. She is killed on their return trip.

María Teresa Mirabal de Guzmán

Born nine years after Minerva, María Teresa is the youngest of the Mirabal sisters. She is the most playful and, until her prison experiences, seemingly the most frivolous of the sisters. She attends Inmaculada Concepción during Minerva's last year at the school. She often covers for Minerva during this year to hide Minerva's subversive activities. María Teresa must eventually bury her first diary because she discusses the school's involvement with Minerva's revolutionary friend Hilda, who is arrested. After her father's death, María Teresa resents him because of his infidelities. She is having romantic difficulties with two of her cousins, who are competing for her affections. She eventually rejects them both, however.

After leaving Inmaculada, she goes to college with Minerva, and she lives with her sister and Manolo during one summer. She is appalled by their small house and witnesses their marital problems. She does not understand their reconciliation until Leandro Guzmán stores guns at their house and they tell her that they are involved in an underground movement. She immediately joins to be near Leandro. She continues her revolutionary activities while at college and marries Leandro in 1958. They have one daughter, Jacqueline. She is arrested in 1960 and shares a cell with Minerva and twenty-two other prisoners. She is miserable in prison, but she learns to adapt, forging a friendship with another prisoner named Magdalena. The prison guards torture her with electrical shocks in front of Leandro in order to secure his cooperation. She secretly writes of this experience to visiting officials of the Organization of American States, who come to investigate Trujillo's prisons. She lives in her mother's house after her release. Leandro is transferred to Puerto Plata prison, and she is killed with her sisters and their driver while returning from a prison visit.

Minerva Mirabal de Tavárez

Minerva is the third Mirabal daughter and the

most committed to revolution. From an early age, she is sharp-tongued and self-confident. She wants to become a lawyer, though her father will not agree to this plan. He does, however, agree to let her attend Inmaculada Concepción with her older sisters. At Inmaculada, she quickly befriends a withdrawn girl named Sinita Perozo. Sinita tells Minerva about the deaths of her male family members. They were murdered for resisting Trujillo. This news shocks Minerva, and she begins the political questioning and fight for justice that will mark her future activities. Minerva, Sinita, and their friends Elsa and Lourdes perform a play before Trujillo, and Sinita aims an arrow at the dictator. Minerva diffuses the situation by chanting "*Viva Trujillo!*"

During her final year at Inmaculada, Minerva befriends a young woman named Hilda, who is a political insurgent. After Hilda is arrested, Minerva must destroy all evidence of their friendship. During her youth, she also meets and becomes interested in Lío Morales. She says she only feels a political kinship with him, but her feelings apparently run deeper than that. She spends three frustrating years at home after graduating. She then discovers that Lío has been writing her letters, which her father has hidden. She also discovers that her father has four other daughters by another woman. She reaches a truce with her father, but she is cold to him. She accepts her half-sisters and even arranges for their education. At a dance, she draws Trujillo's ire when she slaps the dictator for his sexual advances. She accidentally leaves her purse with Lío's letters behind at the dance. Her father is arrested, and she secures his release by apologizing to Trujillo.

Minerva then attends law school, where she meets Manolo Tavárez, whom she marries. They have two children, Minou and Manolito. She earns her law degree, but Trujillo denies her a license to practice. She and Manolo experience marital problems until they become involved in the anti-Trujillo underground movement. She is code-named Mariposa (Butterfly) and is a leader in the movement. After she is arrested in 1960, she retains her resolve in prison and organizes political classes for the women in her cell. She also turns down a pardon because the pardon would indicate that she did something wrong. When she is released, she lives with her mother and loses her political fervor for a time. She regains her resolve when she knows she must work to save her husband and to salvage the fractured underground. She is killed upon returning from her visit with her husband at Puerto Plata prison.

Virgilio Morales

A charismatic young doctor and a Communist revolutionary, Lío becomes close friends with Minerva. Dedé also has a silent infatuation with him. When he must flee the country, he sends Minerva a letter asking her to join him, but Dedé destroys the letter. He and Dedé meet in 1994 and discuss the past and the present state of the country.

Palomino

See Leandro Guzmán

Papá

See Enrique Mirabal

Pedrito

See Pedro Ganzález

Captain Victor Alcinio Peña

Peña is the head of the northern division of the SIM, Trujillo's security force. While the Mirabal sisters are in prison and under house arrest, he visits and keeps strict tabs on the family. He buys Pa-tria's family's farm after the government confiscates it. He helps secure Patria's son Nelson's early release from prison in order to gain the support of the extended González family, who are laborers on the farm. Peña is alternately cruel and accommodating, depending on his purposes.

Sinita Perozo

Sinita attends Inmaculada Concepción after her male relatives are killed for opposing Trujillo. She teaches Minerva about Trujillo's crimes. While performing before the dictator, she points a bow and arrow at him but is stopped by Trujillo's son, Ramfis.

Mercedes Reyes de Mirabal

A very religious and strong woman, Chea Mirabal is the mother of the Mirabal sisters. She tries to protect her family from both outside harm and the harm they may bring on themselves. Her marriage is severely strained after she discovers her husband's long-standing infidelity. In 1960, when her daughters are arrested and Patria loses her farm, most of the family lives with her in her house in town. After the deaths of her daughters, she helps to raise their children. She dies in her sleep twenty years after her daughters' deaths.

Santicló

As a prison guard, Santicló (Santa Clause) receives his nickname by helping the women prisoners. He smuggles in items and delivers communications. He is Margarita Mirabal's cousin.

Manolo Tavárez

Manolo is Minerva's husband. Like her, he is a lawyer, but they are poor and Manolo is unfaithful early in their marriage. Their underground activities bring them closer together, and they both become leaders in the movement. After he is imprisoned, tortured, and loses his wife, he becomes famous in the country. He refuses to run for office, though, and takes to the mountains with a revolutionary force. He and his men are murdered after they surrender on December 21, 1963.

Minou Tavárez

Minou is Minerva's oldest child. She is close to her Mamá Dedé, who helped raise her. In 1994, she is a married woman with a child of her own, Camila.

General Rafael Trujillo

Trujillo is the Dominican dictator who ruled the nation from 1930 until his assassination in 1961. His greed, cruelty, and desire for total control over others inform the lives of all of the characters in the book. He tries to seduce Minerva, but she refuses him. He finally takes his revenge on the rebellious family by ordering the sisters killed.

Themes

Dominican Republic

As Alvarez indicates in her title, *In the Time of the Butterflies*, she is not just concerned with the Mirabal sisters themselves. She is concerned with an era and a way of life. To understand the impact of Trujillo's reign and the significance of the Mirabal sisters, readers must also understand the nation they inhabited. Therefore, Alvarez works to create a sense of the atmosphere of the country, its landscape, its institutions, and its people. The political environment, of course, is one of her chief topics. Trujillo's ruthless regime dominates this time period. By focusing on the country's tribulations over a long period of time, Alvarez communicates the disastrous consequences of Trujillo's rule on a nation and its citizens. She also reveals the changes the country undergoes after Trujillo is assassinated. The epilogue, in particular, stresses the traumas the country has suffered, the changes it has undergone, and the need to remember and learn from the "time of the butterflies."

Authoritarianism

Alvarez uses the Trujillo regime not only to depict the violent methods of this particular dictator but also to reveal the impact of authoritarian governments. Under Trujillo, anyone caught in "subversive" activity—even simply criticizing the government—is subject to imprisonment and, perhaps, torture and death. Dominicans, therefore, live in fear, however muted it may be. They censor what they say to one another, and many also censor their own thoughts. This atmosphere also makes people suspicious of one another, which hinders intimacies and ensures that people suffer in silence. Also, because Trujillo requires that his subjects display his portrait in their homes and that he always be characterized as the nation's hero, he thrusts himself into people's lives. He especially impacts the minds of children, who are taught to hold him on par with religious icons. These authoritarian methods allow dictators to enter and often control almost all spheres of people's lives. Alvarez stresses the consequences of this situation when she has Dedé hear a radio commentator say that dictatorships "are pantheistic. The dictator manages to plant a little piece of himself in every one of us." As Alvarez reveals, such a dictator also manages to satisfy his own monumental desires at the cost of the suffering of thousands.

Change and Transformation

In a novel in which the key word is "butterfly," readers might expect the theme of transformation to be a prominent one. Such is the case with this book. Alvarez focuses on the changes in the Mirabal sisters as they progress toward their revolutionary activities. In addition, she notes the subtle changes taking place in the country while Trujillo is alive.

He comes under criticism from the Catholic Church, and more people join the resistance against him. These elements of the book stress both the dangerous and the liberating qualities of change, whether personally or politically. As Alvarez reveals in characters like Patria and in the country at large, people often must be forcefully thrust out of their patterns of existence, even when those patterns are detrimental. Though change can be painful, it frequently allows individuals or even a nation to discover stronger, richer, and more courageous versions of themselves.

Courage and Cowardice

Clearly, the Mirabal sisters are testaments to the power of courage. In Alvarez's rendering, the sisters also reveal fragility because they are not always courageous and self-assured. Their very fears make them all the more admirable, however, since they overcome them and find the strength to act. They draw strength from one another, as well, revealing that personal fortitude often requires a dependence on others. Bravery may come easier for some, but all of the central characters possess this quality. Minerva's courage is admired by all, but even she suffers from fear and doubt after her release from prison. Dedé, on the other hand, discusses her own lack of boldness when she refuses to join her sisters. She is afraid of losing her marriage, but she also is afraid for herself and for her sisters. Still, in moments of crisis, she also acts bravely to defend others. For instance, when stopped by Trujillo's men while with Minerva, she tells them that she is Minerva in an effort to protect her sister. She also has the courage to continue living after the loss of her sisters. Her nieces and nephews need her strength, and she gives it to them. In 1994, she has the fortitude to look honestly at herself and her country's past.

The courage of the Mirabal sisters is also contrasted with the essential cowardice of Trujillo's men and Trujillo himself, who struts, wears makeup and absurd medals, and constantly must hear about his own superiority. These men hold power and wield it unjustly and brutally. Even when Trujillo is obviously in the wrong, his men carry out his orders to gain favor and prevent their own punishment. Their selfishness and cowardice further highlight the courage of the Mirabal family in resisting such greed and inhumanity.

Topics for Further Study

- Discuss whether writing a fictional account of real people is a valid or fair means of depicting them for an audience. Take into consideration Alvarez's comments in her postscript to *In the Time of the Butterflies*.

- Research the life of a woman who, like the Mirabals, fought for human rights or political change at great personal risk. The list of subjects is quite long, but some possible choices include Harriet Tubman of the Underground Railroad, Qui Jin of China, Ruth First of South Africa, Fannie Lou Hamer of the American Civil Rights Movement, Rigoberta Manchú of Guatemala, or Aung San Suu Kyi of Burma. You also may want to compare people's responses to these women to the Dominican people's responses to the Mirabal sisters.

- Compare the lives of Dominican women today to the lives of Dominican women before 1960. Explore their social positions, gender expectations, educational opportunities, familial roles, or their political impact.

- Compare contemporary political conditions in the Dominican Republic with conditions during the

Trujillo regime.

- Research the relationship between the Trujillo government and the U.S. government. Choose a particular time frame or event that helps to clarify this relationship, and focus on one facet of their relationship, such as their economic ties, their political ties or disputes, or America's role in either maintaining or undermining Trujillo's dictatorship.

- Compare Trujillo's methods of gaining and maintaining power with the methods of another ruler, such as Francisco Franco of Spain, Joseph Stalin of Russia, Mao Tse-Tung of China, Fidel Castro of Cuba, François "Papa Doc" Duvalier of Haiti, or Saddam Hussein of Iraq.

- Construct a psychological profile of a dictator. Discuss his motivations, desires, needs, and possible fears. Address some of the root causes for the dictator's behavior.

- Research the 1937 massacre of Haitians in the Dominican Republic. Examine both its causes and its consequences. Then employ literary works, such as Edwidge Danticat's novel *The Farming of Bones* or Rita Dove's poem "Parsley," to explore how people have reacted to this terrible event.

Family Life

A depiction of family life is central to Alvarez's characterization of the Mirabals because she wants to portray them as Dominican women, not Dominican legends. The Mirabal sisters' families are core elements of their lives. They receive strength and support from their families because, despite their many conflicts, they aid each other even when in disagreement. Of course, their commitments to their families also make the Mirabals vulnerable to painful losses. For instance, Patria grieves over her stillborn child and worries constantly over Nelson after his arrest. The sisters also suffer because of their father's infidelity, although they eventually come to accept their half-sisters. Dedé and Mamá Mirabal suffer acutely when Patria, Minerva, and María Teresa are killed. Alvarez also focuses heavily on the sisters' children. She effectively conveys the sisters' need for them and their willingness to sacrifice for their children's futures. By focusing on the children, Alvarez communicates the powerful loyalties that drive the sisters and cause them both guilt and pain. Without this familial emphasis, Alvarez would not as clearly communicate the sacrifices of the Mirabal family for a cause greater than themselves.

Gender Roles

Alvarez's focus on gender also stresses the achievements of the Mirabal sisters. They live in a country and era in which gender roles are clearly defined. Men hold positions of authority and women largely maintain domestic roles. Alvarez depicts these realities with Enrique Mirabal's attempts to force his daughters to abide by their gender limitations. For instance, he will not allow Minerva to attend law school despite her obvious ability. Alvarez also reveals the consequences of gender definitions through Dedé and Jaimito's marriage. Dedé is very intelligent with a strong business sense, but Jaimito keeps her from exercising these abilities because he wants to "wear the pants" in his family. He tries to maintain his view of masculinity, authority, and honor by running their business affairs, usually with disastrous consequences. Her business success after her divorce testifies to falseness of these gender distinctions.

Alvarez represents the complexity of women's lives by portraying women who challenge gender limitations, such as Minerva and her friends at school, many of whom go on to have successful professional careers. Even Patria, who enjoys the more traditional occupations of wife and mother, becomes involved in revolutionary politics. Alvarez also employs her female characters to depict changes in attitudes toward gender. The Mirabal sisters obviously step outside the boundaries of traditional feminine behavior in the country. Yet, Alvarez also presents the further defiance of the sisters' daughters and even their mother, who advises Minou, Minerva's daughter, to have a career before marrying, although she opposed this desire in Minerva years previously. Ultimately, Alvarez's focus on gender allows her to amplify the range of the Mirabal sisters' challenges and accomplishments in life.

Style

Setting

In the Time of the Butterflies is set in the Dominican Republic. The action takes place between 1938 and 1994, although many of these years are not depicted in the novel. This time period is characterized by Rafael Trujillo's authoritarian rule, which dominates both the country and, quite frequently, people's lives. The Dominican Republic is a largely Catholic country with a very influential Church. The country is also largely patriarchal, with the men holding positions of authority and women most often expected to forego individual careers, although this code is not as rigid as in the past. Trujillo's prisons also are featured prominently in the novel, and Alvarez effectively contrasts their harshness with the general lushness of the country's fertile regions.

Historical Fiction

By creating fictional characters and situations out of historical people and events, Alvarez raises questions about the role of the novel in understanding the past. Does representing actual people in a fictional context diminish their significance—or, worse, constitute unethical misrepresentation? Does changing facts from the era to suit a writer's purposes undermine the messages she is trying to convey? Alvarez addresses these and similar concerns in her postscript to the novel. She never claims historical accuracy in her work. Instead, she asserts that she wanted "to immerse ... readers in an epoch in the life of the Dominican Republic that I believe can only finally be understood by fiction, only finally redeemed by the imagination." Her apparent intent in the work is to convey the emotional and psychological reality of the situation, not strict facts. By fictionalizing, she provides readers with *her* sense of the Mirabal family, the political and social situations in which they lived, and the lessons we can draw from their lives and deaths. For Alvarez, such is the function of a novel, which she says is not "a historical document, but a way to travel through the human heart."

Multiple Points of View

Alvarez tells the Mirabal sisters' stories through their own eyes. Patria, Minerva, and María Teresa narrate three chapters each. Dedé narrates three chapters and the epilogue, which briefly discusses the years between 1960 and 1994. In her postscript to the novel, Alvarez says she began writing the Mirabals' story to understand what gave them their courage to oppose Trujillo's brutal regime. She asserts, though, that "the characters took over, beyond polemics and facts," and she began to invent them. Her use of multiple points of view allows Alvarez to create her fictional Mirabal sisters and to intimately explore the sisters' contrasting personalities. For instance, they each have different motivations for joining or not joining the underground movement against Trujillo, and their individual narratives reveal the development of their political beliefs. They also reveal the quality and depth of their love for others, as well as the difficulties they have maintaining their strength in the face of extreme adversity. This narrative technique helps Alvarez to avoid creating a "mythological" version of the Mirabals that she believes "dismiss[es] the challenge of their courage as impossible for us, ordinary men and women." Her use of individual perspectives, therefore, proves central to generating more human characters who she hopes are "true to the spirit of the real Mirabals."

Diary Entries

María Teresa's chapters consist of her diary entries from her girlhood, young womanhood, and her time in prison. These entries create a far more fragmented picture of events than do the chapters narrated by the other sisters. The diary entries of the younger María Teresa also offer a young girl's perspective on important events in the family's life, such as Patria's child being born dead, Minerva's friendship with the radical Hilda, and her father's death. All three journals contain drawings that reveal María Teresa's emotional and psychological progression. For instance, she draws shoes and a dress in her first journal; in the second, she draws a ring, Minerva's house, and a bomb; in the third, she draws the layout of her prison cell.

Flashbacks

Though the entire book is, in essence, a flashback to the lives of the Mirabals, Dedé's chapters employ this device most explicitly. Her chapters begin with her thoughts and conversations in 1994, then shift back in time when she immerses herself in her memories. This technique emphasizes the impact of the past on the present, as well as the great losses both Dedé and the country have suffered. The flashbacks also offer a contrast between Dedé's desire to keep the past alive and the desire of the country's youth to forget the past entirely.

Sense of Inevitability

By beginning the book with Dedé in 1994, Alvarez foregrounds the Mirabal sisters' deaths from the first chapter. This knowledge colors the reader's experience of the characters and their lives. Even in moments of happiness in the book, the inevitability of the sisters' murders generates a sense of impending doom and loss. It also shifts attention away from questions of plot because the reader does not wonder what will happen to the characters. Instead, the reader is invited to focus on questions of character, character relationships, the reasons behind the Mirabals' fate, and the consequences of their deaths.

Spanish Phrasing

Though she writes the novel in English, Alvarez consistently includes Spanish words or phrases, such as Sor (sister), Tía or Tío (aunt or uncle), por Dios (for Heaven's sake), and El Jefe (The Chief). In his review of the novel, "Sisters in Death" in *The New York Times Book Review*, Roberto González Echevarría contends that Alvarez has "marred" the book with these "Hispanisms" because "Once we accept the idea of English-speaking Mirabals, there is no reason for them to have accents." Isabel Zakrzewski Brown, however, disagrees with this assessment in her article "Historiographic Metafiction in *In the Time of the Butterflies*" in *South Atlantic Review*. She contends that Alvarez's method enables her to create "an artful means of approximating the English-speaking reader to the ambience within which the Mirabal sisters lived."

Historical Context

The Trujillo Regime

The time period of the novel, 1938 to 1994, is dominated by the political regime of dictator Rafael Leonidas Trujillo (1891–1961) and its aftermath. Trujillo ruled the Dominican Republic from 1930 until his assassination in 1961. Before 1930, he had been trained by the American military forces who had taken control of the nation in 1916 and left in 1924. In 1930, he used his position as head of the Dominican military to assume control of the country. To ensure his election as president, his men brutalized political opponents and terrorized voters. He further secured his power by creating a secret police force that violently suppressed opposition to his rule, maintaining networks of spies, and taking control of the press and national education. He took over industries in the country and accumulated an immense fortune. To further trade and strengthen his regime, he supported American business interests in the country and maintained a strong anti-Communist stance.

His reign was characterized by brutality and fear. He regularly employed torture and murder, and the Dominican population was largely terrified of his police forces. The most infamous episode of his dictatorship was the massacre of thousands of Haitian citizens in 1937. Haitian men, women, and children working as sugar-cane cutters or living in Dominican territory were murdered by Trujillo's soldiers. Estimates of the death toll range from 13,000 to 20,000 people.

Trujillo's methods also affected Dominicans' psychological and emotional lives. His presence dominated Dominican life. For instance, he changed the name of the capital city Santo Domingo to Cuidad Trujillo (Trujillo City) in 1936, and he put up signs that read "God and Trujillo." In school, Dominican children were taught to revere him. People were required to hang a picture of Trujillo in their homes. As Alvarez describes in her essay "Genetics of Justice," beneath the picture was the inscription "*In this house Trujillo is Chief.*" People learned to censor themselves and live in fear of reprisals. In the novel, Alvarez quotes a radio commentator who contends that in authoritarian countries, "The dictator manages to plant a little piece of himself in every one of us."

Political Resistance to Trujillo

Though Trujillo's methods of control were highly effective, he could not completely stop either criticism or secret challenges to his rule. He defeated an insurrection attempt in 1949, when exiled Dominicans attempted to overthrow the government. In the 1950s, an underground movement developed. The movement was organized into small eight-to ten-member units or "cells." Many movement members had Communist leanings; others were simply dedicated to ending Trujillo's brutal reign. Exiles tried to invade the country on June 14, 1959, but they failed and were killed. These events spawned the Fourteenth of June Movement, which continued resistance efforts. Both the Mirabal sisters and Alvarez's parents were members of the movement, which planned to assassinate Trujillo in January of 1960. Their plans were uncovered, however, and the movement members either fled or were jailed, tortured, and often killed.

Late in his rule, Trujillo came under increasing international scrutiny. The Catholic Church began to openly criticize Trujillo in 1960. The United States feared his brutality would spawn a revolution directed by Communist rebels or those sympathetic to Fidel Castro, who overthrew Fulgencio Batista's government in Cuba and instituted a Communist regime. The Organization of American States was outraged by Trujillo's attempt to assassinate Venezuelan President Rómulo Betancourt in 1960. Combined with the growing dissatisfaction of wealthier citizens in the Dominican Republic, these elements helped set the stage for Trujillo's downfall. On May 30, 1961, his car was ambushed by some of his former supporters and he was shot to death. Alvarez reveals in "Genetics of Justice" that Dominicans call his death not an assassination but an "*ajusticiamiento*, a bringing to justice." Indeed, the anniversary of his death is now a national holiday in the country.

The Post-Trujillo Era

Dominican politics continued to be marked by corruption after Trujillo's demise. In 1962, Juan Bosch defeated Joaquín Balaguer, who had been president under Trujillo, in the presidential elections. Bosch's liberal reforms were opposed by the United States and the Dominican military, however. Bosch was ousted by the military after only months in office. The years that followed contained further discord, including rigged elections and civil war. In 1965, the United States sent in Marines to occupy the country; in 1966, Balaguer again became president in a corrupt election. Balaguer was president until 1978, then was re-elected in 1986 and served until 1996, despite being almost ninety years old and nearly blind and deaf. From 1960 to 1994, when the novel ends, political and economic reform remained elusive for the country.

Dominican Culture and Economy

The culture in which the Mirabals live also contains restrictions and expectations not directly linked to Trujillo. The Dominican Republic is a predominantly Catholic country. Catholic beliefs and rituals inform the lives of everyone in the novel, even those who are not overtly religious. The people also hold widespread views about the roles of men and women in society. Alvarez's characters often speak of the male "macho" ethic, wherein a man must prove his strength, courage, and ability to run his own life and family. Contrasted to this ethic are the roles of women, which the Mirabal sisters often challenge. Women are expected to maintain primarily domestic lives as wives and mothers, although those limitations are not insurmountable. In the 1950s and 1960s, women were attending universities in the country, and many were assuming professional careers. The pressures to marry and bear children still impacted their lives, however.

Compare & Contrast

- **1960:** Trujillo rules the country. No opposition party exists. No genuine elections are held. Joaquín Balaguer is Trujillo's puppet president.

  1996: Balaguer steps down from the presidency. He held the office from 1966 to 1978 and from 1986 to 1996, winning in rigged elections. The new president, Leonel Fernandez Reyna, is elected with Balaguer's support. The election is judged non-corrupt. His vice-president is Jaime David Fernandez Mirabal, Dedé Mirabal's son. Patria Mirabal's son Nelson Gonzalez Mirabal is the vice-president's chief aid. Minerva Mirabal's daughter Minou Tavares Mirabal is deputy foreign minister.

- **1960:** A 137-foot obelisk stands in Cuidad Trujillo. The dictator erected it in his own honor.
  1999: The obelisk in the renamed Santo Domingo is adorned with a mural of the four Mirabal sisters. It is a monument to all who struggled for liberty in the country.

- **1960:** On November 25, Patria, Minerva, and Marí Teresa Mirabal are killed under Trujillo's orders.
  1999: November 25 has been designated the International Day against Violence against Women in the Mirabals' honor.

Economically, the country has often struggled because of its reliance on agricultural exports that are subject to fluctuations in commodity prices. Farmers produce primarily sugar, but they also export coffee, cocoa beans, and tobacco. The economy also depends on mining exports, especially gold and silver. In the 1980s and 1990s, tourism has taken an increasingly central role in the country, becoming second in revenues only to agriculture. In fact, in the novel Dedé contends that the country has become "the playground of the Caribbean."

Critical Overview

Since its release in 1994, *In the Time of the Butterflies* has received largely positive reviews. Most critics praise Alvarez for bringing the Mirabal sisters' story to an American audience unfamiliar with their lives, struggles, and deaths. In their reviews of the novel, critics such as Janet Jones Hampton, Brad Hooper, Rebecca S. Kelm, and Kay Pritchett also comment on Alvarez's ability to effectively portray her characters' personal and domestic lives. Hampton, Hooper, and Pritchett commend Alvarez's focus on the political elements of her story. Pritchett, for example, contends in *World Literature Today* that Alvarez adeptly balances "the political and the human, the tragic and the lyrical." She also lauds Alvarez's style, which she says "seems to emerge from the core of woman's experience, passion, and grief."

Not all critics view the novel so favorably, however. Barbara Mujica and Roberto González Echevarría, for instance, find many areas of weakness in the work. Mujica asserts in *Americas* that Alvarez actually goes too far in humanizing her characters, making them "Smaller-than-life." She also believes that the characters "are rather too formulaic and unidimensional to hold our attention," which may hinder readers from reaching the more compelling passages in the latter stages of the book, areas in which "Alvarez has much to tell us about the strength of the human will."

In his important review in *The New York Times Book Review*, González Echevarría views Alvarez's characterizations differently. He believes that Alvarez "did not escape the temptation to monumentalize" the Mirabal sisters, which hurts the novel. In addition, he characterizes the Mirabal sisters as "reactive and passive," saying that Alvarez portrays them "as earnestly innocent and vulnerable, but that diminishes their political stature and fictional complexity." The world that Alvarez creates, according to González Echevarría, also includes "far too many misdeeds and misfortunes" while still failing to make the reader aware "of a broader, more encompassing political world."

Other significant reviews disagree with González Echevarría's evaluation of the novel. Ilan Stavans commends the book in *Nation* and, unlike González Echevarría, he does not see the Mirabal sisters as passive. Instead, they offer a potent challenge to their society. Stavans asserts that Alvarez takes a unique approach to the Trujillo era by examining "the martyrdom of these three Dominican women as a gender battlefield." The sisters are raised in a chauvinistic society, confront the limitations this society places on women, and are killed by a dictator who must constantly demonstrate masculine power. For Stavans, though, the prominence of the Mirabals is balanced by the overarching presence of Trujillo, who is such a pervasive figure that Stavans says, "it seems to me he becomes the central character."

In *The Women's Review of Books*, Ruth Behar

also comments on Alvarez's feminist approach to her topic. Behar believes that Alvarez joins other Latina writers "in the feminist quest to bring Latin American women into the nation and into history as agents," not merely as passive figures under male dominance. Behar also examines Alvarez's portrayal of the power of dictators to assert themselves in everyone's lives. She also considers Alvarez's treatments of history and revolution in the book. Behar holds that "This is a historical novel in which forgetting wins out over remembering. Alvarez offers a paradox: her novel bears witness to the urgency of her quest for memory, but for her characters healing comes only through forgetting." She criticizes Alvarez for not fully considering the corruption of revolutionaries turned dictators, but ultimately she compliments her for "showing that although revolutions turn sour, they matter."

Two critical articles have been printed on the novel. The first is "Recovering a Space for a History between Imperialism and Patriarchy: Julia Alvarez's *In the Time of the Butterflies*" by Elizabeth Coonrod Martínez, and the second is "Historiographic Metafiction in *In the Time of the Butterflies*" by Isabel Zakrzewski Brown. As do Stavans and Behar, Martínez compares Alvarez to other contemporary Latina and Chicana writers who focus on gender conflicts and represent Latin American history through women's lives. Martínez contends that like other Latin American women writers, Alvarez portrays the two sexes joined together in a common struggle, not separated by individual agendas. She also praises Alvarez for humanizing the Mirabal sisters while still constructing a political message that criticizes other nations, including America, for complicity with the Trujillo regime.

Brown also examines the feminist issues in the novel. Her approach, however, is historical. She treats the novel within the context of "historiographic metafiction," a term coined by critic Linda Hutcheon to describe the self-aware uses of history in contemporary novels. A significant portion of her article is dedicated to comparing Alvarez's fictional representations with the existing biographies of the Mirabals, detailing Alvarez's transformations of fact. She ultimately criticizes Alvarez for fashioning the Mirabal sisters into stereotypes and being "unable to avoid the mythification process she had professed to elude."

What Do I Read Next?

- Like *In the Time of the Butterflies*, Alvarez's first novel, *How the*

García Girls Lost Their Accents (1991), revolves around the lives of four sisters. In this semi-autobiographical work, she depicts their struggles both as Dominican immigrants to the United States and as women.

- *Something to Declare*, published in 1998, is a collection of personal essays by Alvarez. She discusses several aspects of her life, including her search for information about the Mirabal sisters in "Chasing the Butterflies" and the impact of Trujillo on her family in "Genetics of Justice".

- *The Woman Warrior* (1976) by Maxine Hong Kingston inspired Alvarez. This acclaimed work is based on Kingston's experiences. It foregrounds Chinese cultural expectations, such as the imposition of gender restrictions and the perceived dangers of storytelling, with which contemporary Chinese-American women must contend.

- Edwidge Danticat's 1998 novel *The Farming of Bones* employs fiction to portray the impact of Trujillo's 1937 massacre of Haitian immigrants in the Dominican Republic.

- In her poem "Parsley," Rita Dove

evokes the horror of Trujillo's 1937 massacre and constructs a psychological portrait of the dictator. She focuses on the test Trujillo's men used to determine who would be killed: a person's ability to properly pronounce the Spanish word for parsley.

- *The Inhabited Woman* by Nicaraguan writer Gioconda Belli tells the story of a successful woman, Lavinia, who is influenced by the spirit of a female Indian warrior to rebel against both gender restrictions and her country's military dictatorship. This title was translated by Kathleen March in 1994.

- Gabriel García Márquez's novel *The Autumn of the Patriarch* is a psychological study of a cruel, lonely, and paranoid Latin American dictator. Employing a complex structure and a "stream-of-consciousness" style, the book is challenging to read. The first U.S. edition appeared in 1976 and was translated by Gregory Rabassa.

- In his famous work *The Prince*, which appeared in English in 1907, Niccolo Machiavelli details the means of sustaining political power.

The work is known for its disregard for abstract rights and morality in favor of practical, brutal solutions to political problems.

- Adolf Hitler wrote *Mein Kampf* (translated as *My Battle*) before he rose to power in Germany. The book provides a frightening insight into racial hatred and Hitler's prescription for maintaining an authoritarian society.

Sources

Julia Alvarez, "A Brief Account of My Writing Life," *Appalachian State University Summer Reading Program*, http://www.geocities.com/CollegePark/Library/4061 varez.html, 1997.

Julia Alvarez, "Genetics of Justice," in her *Something to Declare*, Algonquin Books of Chapel Hill, 1998, pp. 103-11.

Ruth Behar, "Revolutions of the Heart," *The Women's Review of Books*, May, 1995, pp. 6-7.

Jonathan Bing, "Julia Alvarez: Books that Cross Borders," *Publishers Weekly*, Vol. 243, No. 51, pp. 38-39.

Isabel Zakrzewski Brown, "Historiographic Metafiction in *In the Time of the Butterflies*," *South Atlantic Review*, Spring, 1999, pp. 98-112.

Roberto González Echevarría, "Sisters in Death," *The New York Times Book Review*, December 18, 1994, p. 28.

Elizabeth Coonrod Martínez, "Recovering a Space for a History between Imperialism and Patriarchy: Julia Alvarez's *In the Time of the Butterflies,*" *Thamyris*, Autumn, 1998, pp. 263-79.

Barbara Mujica, a review in *Americas*, March-April, 1995, p. 60.

Kay Pritchett, a review in *World Literature Today*,

Autumn, 1995, p. 789.

Ilan Stavans, "Las Mariposas," *Nation*, November 7, 1994, pp. 552-56.

For Further Study

Julia Alvarez, "Chasing the Butterflies," in her *Something to Declare*, Algonquin Books of Chapel Hill, 1998, pp. 197-209.

> In this essay, Alvarez describes her attempts to find information on the Mirabal sisters and her progress toward writing a novel about them.

Aurora Arias, "The Mirabal Sisters," *Connexions*, Vol. 39, 1992, pp. 4-5.

> This article gives a brief account of the Mirabal family, focusing most prominently on Minerva.

Janet Jones Hampton, a review in *Belles Lettres: A Review of Books by Women*, Spring, 1995, pp. 6-7.

> Hampton praises the novel and identifies is overriding theme as "every person's accommodation of injustice."

Brad Hooper, a review in *Booklist*, July, 1994, p. 1892.

> Hooper's one paragraph review is positive and says that the novel effectively balances domestic and political drama.

Rebecca S. Kelm, a review in *Library Journal*, August, 1994, p. 123.

In this very brief review, Kelm highly recommends the book and praises Alvarez for focusing on the characters' personal lives.

Susan Miller, "Family Spats, Urgent Prayers," *Newsweek*, October 17, 1994, p. 77.

Miller commends Alvarez for her character depictions and compares her to Denise Chavez.

Review in *Publishers Weekly*, July 11, 1994, p. 62.

This anonymous review asserts that while the novel begins slowly, it eventually reaches "a gripping intensity." It also claims that Marí Teresa's story begins as the least engaging then grows into the most moving of the four sisters' tales.

Heather Rosario-Sievert, "Conversation with Julia Alvarez," *Review: Latin American Literature and Arts*, Spring, 1997, pp. 31-37.

In this interview, Alvarez discusses her writing background, her challenges as a Latina writer, her sources of inspiration, and her view of the Dominican Republic.

Ava Roth, "Sisters in Revolution," *Ms. Magazine*, September-October, 1994, pp. 79-80.

Roth describes how Alvarez details the Mirabal sisters' many rebellions. She believes that Alvarez provides a story that is as much inspiration as tragedy.

Printed by BoD in Norderstedt, Germany